Seven types of the Chinese teas
Or how to distinguish one from another

By Alisson Evans

Contents:

Introduction

I'm sure that this book will be especially useful
to those who very little knowledge about the
Chinese teas and still completely haven't
understood all these unclear terms. I will try to
explain with simple words to you what are the
Chinese teas are and to accurately classify all
this.

Photo by Wei Tang

Seven types of teas

In China, there are seven types of teas.
Here they:
1. Green teas.
2. White teas.
3. Yellow teas.
4. Oolong teas.
5. Red teas.
6. Black teas.
7. Pu-erh teas.

Each of these types is like a direction. Each group comprises a huge variety of teas. So, for example, Green teas - great variety. Also, there are a lot of White teas and Oolong teas too.

What do teas from different types differ in? First, raw materials. The tea leaf for each of these types gathers from certain tea-plants. One species of tea-plants are suitable for green grades of tea. Other tea-plants are for Oolong teas, for example. For Red teas are the third tea-plants, and so on. Today in China more than 260 kinds of tea-plants of a *Camellia sinensis* are known.

And secondly, a way of processing. The way of processing of a tea leaf differs from type-to-type. And I show it on each of them now, so it will be more clear to you.

Green tea

It is, perhaps, the most popular tea in China. It is grown up in many provinces of Celestial Empire. Also, there is truly a huge number of kinds of green teas. All of them in a varying degree differ from each other, but at the same time are united in one group of green teas, because the methods of their processing are very similar. Green tea is almost not fermented tea. Its processing takes several hours. And it is practically not exposed to mechanical influence. Conjure with him accurately and with love. The sense of green tea is in as much as possible to keep the integrity of a leaf. And visually the quality of green tea is determined by as far as virgin soils and his leaf is beautiful. For this reason, green tea is never packed into a vacuum. Practically all green teas are produced not from a tea leaf, namely from a kidney – the most top young boring. They are labor-consuming assembled and very gentle. Green teas have pronounced flower aromas, wonderful tastes, and the richest aftertastes. Good green tea – it is divinely pleasant!

It is wrong to consider that everything that green color, is green tea. No, it not so. White teas, Yellow teas, and light Oolong – too green in color. But they don't treat the type of green teas.

White tea

White tea is shockingly delightful! It is beautiful so that I can talk about it for hours. But with it, there is one feature. It is necessary to grow to him nevertheless. It is clearly not at once and not all. The Chinese white teas have the delicate aroma and the most delicate taste. In the flower, fruit, and honey notes sparkle. And then all this comes back and covers with a scattering of diamond aftertaste. If you smoke, you won't feel it. If you have had dinner sharp chicken wings from McDonald's, you will also not feel it. The Chinese white teas are very clean. It is necessary to be the same clean in reply. It is necessary to want them to understand. But if you understand them, then, more carefully, you can become dependent.

White tea is grown up only in several provinces in China. Also, he gathers from certain bushes. One of the most widespread species of tea-plants for production "white" are 政和大白茶 (Zhenghe Da Baicha) и 福鼎大白茶 (Fuding Da Baicha) .

A feature of these tea-plants is that the tea kidney is covered with the white pile. From here and the name of the tea.

The way of production of white teas differs essentially. They are practically not processed. White tea is removed from a bush and dried up in the sun. That's all. It isn't subjected to either mechanical nor heat treatment. It is not fermented tea. And it keeps in himself all force of the southern sun, all power, and all juice. White teas quite strongly differ from each other in appearance (so, for example, Baihao Yinzhen isn't similar to Gongmei at all), but nevertheless even at a glance without effort it is possible to establish that the white, on this down on kidneys.

Photo by Petai Jantrapoon

Yellow teas

Yellow tea is the Chinese elite. Teas are with very deep, various aromas. These teas are grown up in five provinces in China. And each of these provinces produces own yellow tea. Yellow teas are united by one common feature in the course of production. This stage is called "languor". After the tea leaf was collected, dried, warmed up and missed", it is wrapped in special hygroscopic paper in the small portions on 0.5 kg, and then removed on several tens of hours to the dark and warm place. During this time tea "turns yellow". This production stage gives tea a recognizable, specific aroma and smacks which distinguishes him from other types of teas. Externally yellow teas are similar to some types of white teas and to green teas. But, with certain experience, you without effort will be able to distinguish one from another.

Yellow teas are produced only from the top kidneys. These are teas obviously expensive. And often it is very expensive. It is elite. Their aroma bewitches. These are delightful slight flower emotions, and these are always major notes. Whatever of types of yellow tea you have taken, it will always be elastic, bright and incendiary.

Oolong teas

Many understand not at once what is Oolong tea, and mistakenly consider that it is some grade of tea. Actually, it not so. I will explain. Oolong tea is the whole group of teas. Oolong tea is grown up in the southern provinces of China. And each of these provinces makes own grades of Oolong tea. For example, there are Guangdong Oolong tea is the Oolong which is grown up in the Province of Guangdong. Or the southern Fujian Oolong tea is the Oolong which is grown up in the south of a Province of Fujian. (Legendary Tieguanyin concerns them). Or still, for example, the North Fujian Oolong tea (these are well-known for Dahongpao, Shuixian, and Rougui).

Oolong teas exist a huge set. And each type of Oolong tea is collected from the species of a bush. For example, for Tieguanyin it 毛蟹 (Maoxie) . And for Dahongpao it 大红袍 (Da, Hong Pao).

Oolong tea it is essentially possible to divide into two subgroups. There is nothing difficult, but nevertheless - attention! These are light Oolong tea and dark Oolong tea. All those that green color belong to light. Too dark - dark. Tieguanyin – light Oolong tea. Dahongpao – dark.

At light Oolong tea, the freshness is a critical indicator. They are stored in vacuum packings and in refrigerators at a temperature of-18C. At dark Oolong tea, the freshness has no value. And many Chinese, on the contrary, consider that than dark Oolong tea is more senior, it is richer with that. They are stored at room temperature, and the only requirement is that the room was dry. (The southeast Chinese humidity is the main enemy of tea).

What unites these such different teas in one group? Of course, a way of production. All Oolong teas are the semi-fermented teas. And in the course of production great comes the way of them! Besides, Oolong teas are made not from kidneys, namely from a tea leaf. From the first, the second, third, fourth, and sometimes and the fifth from above leaflets.

So, as the production process looks. At first, they are aired in the open air until leaves don't begin to redden at the edges. Then they are unloaded in bass bamboo drums and actively twisted within 15-20 minutes. Then they are spread on trays and removed to the dark room on all night long. Next day they begin to be rumpled. Oolong teas rumple actively and ruthlessly. By special equipment, machines and manually. They are wrapped in "spheres", broken, pressed, rumpled hands and so on …

The sense of all these manipulations is in releasing the maximum quantity of juice from a tea leaf and to oxidize it for the minimum quantity of time. Thus, Oolong tea is the semi-fermented tea. Then the tea leaf is fried thoroughly in special furnaces. It is dried up. "Is fixed". And further oxidation stops. After that it is necessary only to touch tea, to take from it all branches, scapes and to separate clean tea leaves. "tea aunts" still long-term after the end of a tea season are engaged in it.

It is obvious that light Oolong tea is fried thoroughly much less, than dark. From here and color.

Oolong teas are a great variety. And, respectively, a great variety of their tastes and aromas.

Oolong teas whatever they were - dark or light - it is always bright, fresh and is young! Oolong teas drive! These are the most vital teas.)

Red tea

It is the tea, most widespread in the world. In India, on Ceylon, and in Kenya – to manufacture red teas. We buy red teas in our supermarkets, in the same countries calling them black. But the Chinese red teas essentially differ from all what can be bought in the shop around the corner in the packaged look. What is difference in? In everything.

At the Chinese, Red teas are another color. And other taste. And another aroma. And absolutely another fortress, and amount of tea leaves. The Chinese Red teas are Red teas number one in the world. I am not subjective now. I am devilishly objective. Trust me.

Teas from shops for mass consumption land by machines, gather by machines and are processed by machines. They have sprayed pesticides and generously fertilized. They are blended in huge volumes and packed up in the cool, thought-over packing. They are loaded with advertising and marketing, and then they rigidly fight for the best regiments in supermarkets.

With the Chinese red teas all a little in a different way. To the Yunnan farmers in general on drumming the outside world. They do Red teas because their father did Red teas, their grandfather did Red teas too, and the great-grandfather did Red teas too. They own hectares of plantations, annually reap from them a crop and process everything manually on the self-made equipment and in furnaces on firewood. They don't compete with world leaders. They, in general, see the world in another plane.

Red Chinese teas are produced in 12 provinces of Celestial Empire. But those that are grown up in the Provinces of Yunnan and Fujian are the most known. Red teas are the strongly fermented teas. In the course of production, they are processed both mechanically, and thermally, and steamed, and dried thoroughly. It is a difficult process which takes several days. During this time the tea leaf almost completely is oxidized, darkens, and then and grows brown. You shouldn't take the name of Red teas literally. Of course, they are not such red, like a Chinese flag. But at the exit, we receive tea of dark-brown color.

At tea leaves, the Chinese Red teas give the magic color of infusion. You are surprised by his beauty if you make such tea in glassware and look at the light.

It as if shines in cozy claret color from within.
These teas have a deep velvety aroma. They are
pleasant to adult men. They can be made strong.
They warm. And they are especially good in the
evening.

Red teas "clear" and "honest". All without any
exception.

Photo by Natthapon Ngamnithiporn

Black teas

Black tea is produced in the Provinces of Hunan, Hubei, Guangxi, and Sichuan. It is not such popular tea in the domestic market of China, but nevertheless, he has the consumer. Black tea is really black. And in the course of the processing becomes completely fermented. For a hundred percent.

To these leaves gets most of all from the hands of tea masters. The process of production of black tea, perhaps, the most difficult and long. At first, the leaf passes several stages of airing and twisting. Then it is rumpled and squeezes out the juice. And then fill up in huge bunkers and heat them. In these bunkers under the influence of temperature and moisture tea is actively fermented during tens of hours. At the exit, he becomes absolutely black and soft. Then it is dried. And then also press. Black tea is traditionally pressed in the form of tiles or in the form of cylinders.

Black tea gives brown, dark infusion and has pronounced aroma. At its aroma, there are a tartness, viscosity, fruit notes and "rural smells". It is ambiguous, special and quite local tea which you understand not from the first and which isn't on sale in any shop. It is interesting. And, I would tell, is extravagant. It at least.

Pu-erh teas

Pu-erh teas allocate in the separate type of the Chinese teas. Because with them there is one serious feature. They are two essentially excellent types. It is green – Shen Pu-erh. And dark - Shiu Pu-erh. And now I, in brief, will tell about each of them.

But before I should tell that only those teas which are grown up and produced in the Province of Yunnan can be called Pu-erhs. It is the southern province of China bordering on Tibet. If the manufactory on the production of tea costs in several kilometers on that side of the border – all - such teas won't be considered as Pu-erh teas anymore. And the manufactory isn't certified. Yes, it is the state patronage.

For the production of Pu-erh teas use the biggest leaves. It is considered that the more the leaf, the is the higher quality of Pu-erh. The most expensive and magnificent kinds of this tea are made from a leaf of tea trees. Not bushes, namely trees. In the Province of Yunnan gardens from such tea, trees meet, externally they are similar to apple or pear orchards. Farmers by means of ladders collect from them a tea leaf, process it and hand over these raw materials on factories where already directly press pancakes.

勐海大叶茶 (Camellia Sinensis Var assarmica CV. Menghai Daye Cha) -is an example of the botanical name of one of the most widespread species of a tea tree for production of Pu-erhs. It is important to tell that in most cases Pu-erhs press at a final production phase. For this reason on sale, we often see them in the form of "pancakes", "bricks", "nests", "tiles" and so on. Seldom, but nevertheless also weight Pu-erh meets. Why is this type of tea pressed? It has so developed historically. It wasn't really convenient to Ancient Chinese logistic companies to transport large and easy volumes of freights. Therefore they asked producers to press tea. Such tradition has remained up to now.

Pu-erh is incredibly ancient tea. His history is thousands of years. The modern market for Pu-erh teas – is huge and interesting. It and pirates, and fake teas, both excess profits, and even state lobby. In the Province of Yunnan thousands and thousands of certified plants and factories on the production of Pu-erhs are concentrated. And as much again not certified small-scale productions.

So, as I already spoke, in Pu-erhs there are two directions.

These are light Shen Pu-erh. And dark Shiu Pu-erh. Technologies of their production are various.

We will begin with light teas. Farmers remove a leaf for production light Shen Pu-erhs from tea trees, then slightly dry it in the sun, then process on fire in big metal "woks". Then dry up, touch and unload in huge bags. Such raw materials are called "maocha". The plants and manufactories buy up these raw materials at farmers and on special technology press, it informs.

In light Shen Pu-erhs the defining factor is the quality of initial raw materials. Than trees from which have collected a leaf, then more leaf are more senior and what has located a plantation above, the quality of tea will be better for those, the aroma is brighter, taste is strong.

Every year storages light Shen Pu-erhs become more dark, wiser and denser. They get new shades of aroma and taste. And their cost grows approximately by 25% a year. It is considered that the Pu-erh, the better is more senior. "Young" teas Shen Pu-erhs are objectively not so good as five-six-year-old. Shen Pu-erhs sustained 5-6 years are considered as optimum based on the ratio of the price and quality.

They aren't so expensive, but in their taste, the bitterness and tartness peculiar from "young" Shen to Pu-erhs almost completely leave. 12-15-year-old Shen Pu-erhs are considered as an exclusive and cost really much. If suggest buying to you 12-year Pu-erh for 160 dollars is obviously deception. Be not tempted. 20-25-year Pu-erhs are already "other orbit".

At the same time, you have to understand that the term of endurance is important, but not defining factor. The quality of initial raw materials is defining nevertheless. It is more important than the rest.

Shen Pu-erhs are fantastically tasty and interesting. Aroma of this tea incredibly saturated. It is the whole world! These teas tone up, load and warm!

Dark Shiu Pu-erhs. They began to be made relatively recently. In the seventies. And the technology of their production differs from the production of any other tea. What here occurs? When farmers hand over raw materials on tea factories, at factories pour these raw materials in huge heaps. Then they are plentifully watered and covered with special fabric. At the same time densely press fabric at the edges stones. At this moment process of "the accelerated fermentation" is started.

What is going on? Speaking very roughly, a heap of tea raw materials begins to decay. It sounds bad, but so. The tea leaf under the influence of microorganisms is great warmed and begins to darken. Once a day here the worker with a pitchfork comes and properly stirs this heap in order that process of fermentation went evenly. And so 45 days proceed. Sometimes it is slightly more. The chief of tea production at factory independently makes the decision on when to stop the process. For these 45 days, dark Shiu Pu-erh passes in the mode of such "the accelerated fermentation" approximately the same stages, as light Shen Pu-erh in 30 years of endurance on the shelf. Thus, the production technology of dark Shiu Pu-erh as much as possible brings closer him to sustained Shen Pu-erh. But there is an important point. Brings closer! But doesn't do it just the same. It should be understood.

It is considered that dark Shiu Pu-erh becomes, in the same way, better from year to year. Though these changes aren't so obvious, as at light Shen Pu-erhs. Dark Shiu Pu-erh young people can drink. And even absolutely fresh Shiu Pu-erh who have pressed in a pancake of all a few days ago will be already quite good.

It is important to tell that dark Shiu Pu-erh
practically is never made from expensive raw
materials. For their production, the ordinary tea
leaf from rather young plantations is used. For
the same reason, dark Shiu Pu-erh much rarer is
subject to collecting, in comparison with light
Shen Pu-erhs.

Shiu Pu-erh gives dark, almost black color of
infusion. It is dense, velvety tea with the same
dense and velvety aroma. In aroma of this tea
"rural notes" and "earthiness" often dominate.
Beginners are often confused by such smells, but
after you get used to them, it doesn't become
simple to come off this tea anymore.

Chinese believe that they of Shiu Pu-erh
positively affect digestion, work of the digestive
tract and promote weight loss. Any doctor of
traditional Chinese medicine will confirm these
words. Shiu Pu-erh teas are considered as the
most correct teas from the point of view of
health.
Probably, it is necessary to tell that in the
Province of Yunnan the highest life expectancy
in China. It is statistics.

Shiu Pu-erh is a tea which should be known.
Today it is the most popular of the Chinese teas
in the European market.

Epilogue
So, I summarize.
There are seven groups of the Chinese teas. We
will repeat once again.
It: green, yellow, white, oolong, red, black and
Pu-erh. That Oolong happens light and dark.
And it is very different teas though they also
belong to one group. Still, we have learned that
Pu-erhs have two "directions" - it is light Shen
Pu-erh and dark Shiu Pu-erh which are made on
absolutely various technologies.
Still, we have learned that each tea gathers from
certain species of tea trees, is processed by
techniques excellent from each other and grown
up in various provinces.

And still that tastes and aromas at each of
groups differ from each other in a time radically.
But each tea is in own way magnificent.

In modern China, there are more than 900 types
of tea.

The Chinese teas are a huge world of tastes,
aromas, flowers, and forms. The Chinese teas are
incredibly refined subject. But if someone tells
you that it is difficult, don't trust! It isn't more
difficult to understand the Chinese teas, than
any other subject.

Dear readers!
I am immensely grateful to you for the fact that
you have read my book.
I wrote it for you with the purpose that everyone
could better understand what Chinese tea is.
It would be very pleasant to me for your honest
review of the book. It is my first book which I
have decided to write after several years of life
in China - the amazing country.
I hope you had a good time behind reading!

Pleasant reading and tea drinking,
Your Alisson.